ENGLISH/GERMAN

The Toddler's Handbook

With over 100 Words that every kid should know

By Dayna Martin

ENGLISCH/DEUTSCH

ENGAGE BOOKS
VANCOUVER

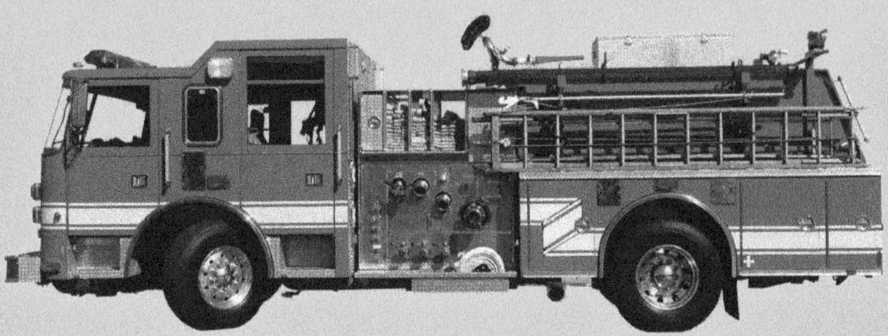

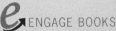

ENGAGE BOOKS

THIRD EDITION / FIRST PRINTING

Mailing address
PO BOX 4608
Main Station Terminal
349 West Georgia Street
Vancouver, BC
Canada, V6B 4A1

www.engagebooks.ca

Written & compiled by: Dayna Martin
Edited & translated by: A.R. Roumanis
Proofread by: Susanne Lehmann, Jeffrey Hurni, Christoph Scheps and Christian Leuschner
Consultation by: Jennifer Johnson and Danielle DenAdmirant
Designed by: A.R. Roumanis
Photos supplied by: Shutterstock
Photo on page 47 by: Faye Cornish

LIBRARY AND ARCHIVES CANADA CATALOGUING IN PUBLICATION

Martin, Dayna, 1983–, author
The toddler's handbook: with over 100 words that every kid should know : English/German / by Dayna Martin.

Issued in print and electronic formats.
Text in English and German.
ISBN 978-1-77226-237-7 (bound). –
ISBN 978-1-77226-236-0 (paperback). –
ISBN 978-1-77226-238-4 (pdf). –
ISBN 978-1-77226-239-1 (epub). –
ISBN 978-1-77226-240-7 (kindle)

1. German language – Vocabulary – Juvenile literature.
2. Vocabulary – Juvenile literature.
I. Martin, Dayna, 1983– . Toddler's handbook.
II. Martin, Dayna, 1983– . Toddler's handbook. German.
III. Title.

PF3445.M37 2016 J438.1 C2015-907731-1
C2015-907732-X

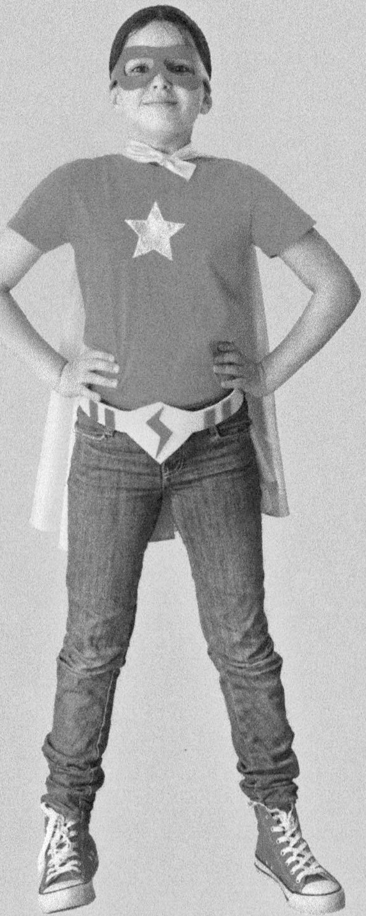

Aa

der Alligator

Alligator

der Bär

Bb

Bear

die Katze

Cc

Cat

der Hund

Dd

Dog

der Elefant

Ee

Elephant

der Fuchs

Ff

Fox

die Ziege

Gg

Goat

das Pferd

Hh

Horse

der Leguan

Ii

Iguana

der Jaguar

Jj

Jaguar

der Koala

Kk

Koala

der Löwe

Ll

Lion

die Maus

Mm

Mouse

der Wassermolch

Nn

Newt

der Otter

Oo

Otter

das Schwein

Pp

Pig

die Wachtel

Qq

Quail

der Hase

Rr

Rabbit

die Robbe

Ss

Seal

der Tiger

Tt

Tiger

der Uakari

Uu

Uakari

der Geier

Vv

Vulture

das Wiesel

Ww

Weasel

der Sternflecksalmler

Xx

X-ray fish

das Yak

Yy

Yak

das Zebra

Zz

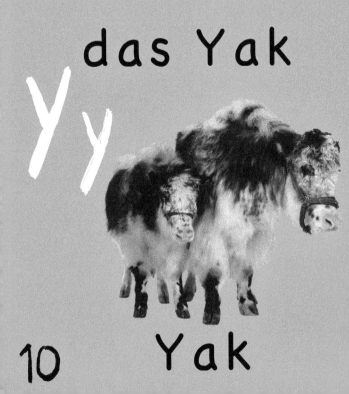

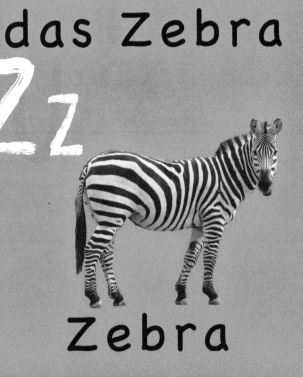

Zebra

der Apfel

eins
1
One

Apple

die Kräcker

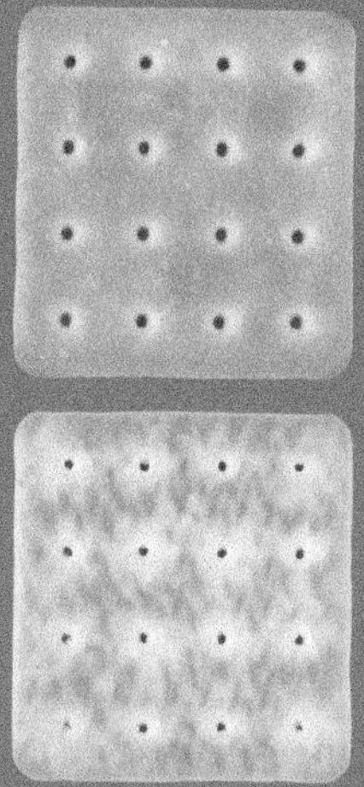

zwei
2
Two

Crackers

die Wassermelonen

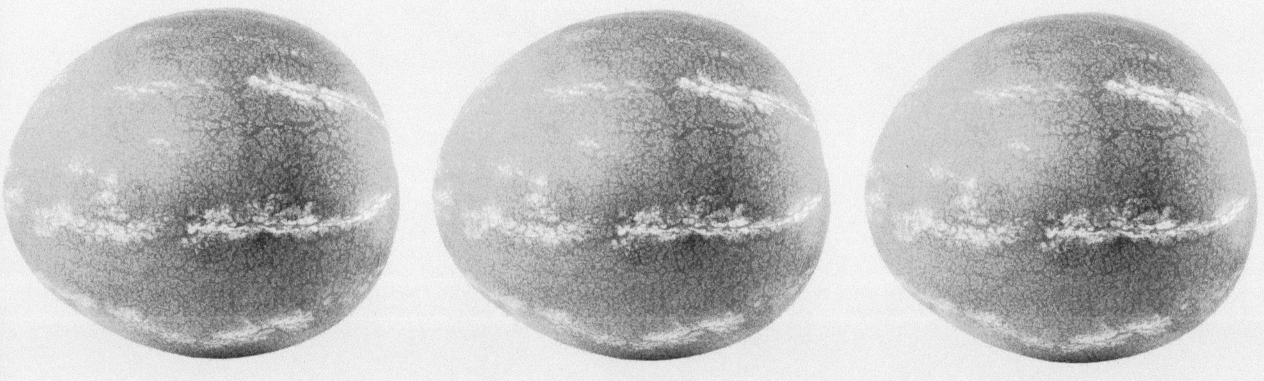

drei
3
Three

Watermelons

die Erdbeeren

vier

4

Four

Strawberries

die Karotten

fünf

5

Five

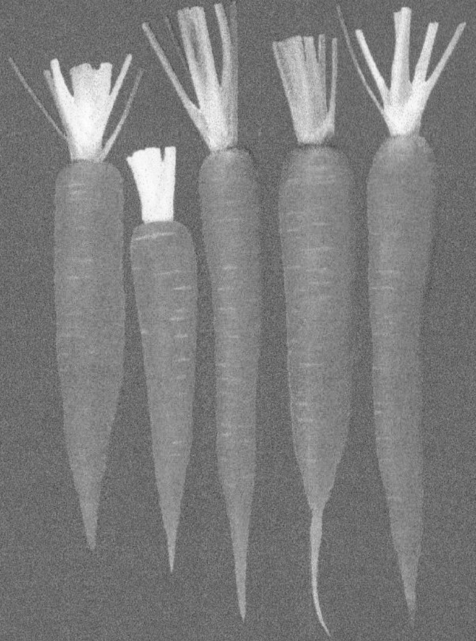

Carrots

die Tomaten

sechs

6

Six

Tomatoes

die Kürbisse

sieben

7

Seven

Pumpkins

die Früchte

acht

8

Eight

Fruit slices

die Kartoffeln

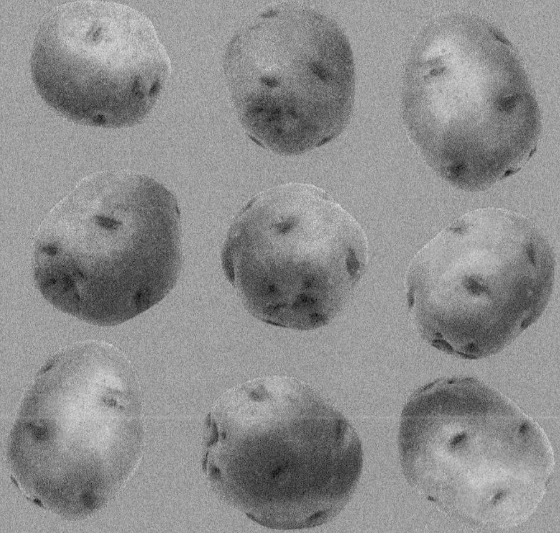

neun

9

Nine

Potatoes

die Kekse

zehn

10

Ten

Cookies

der Regenbogen

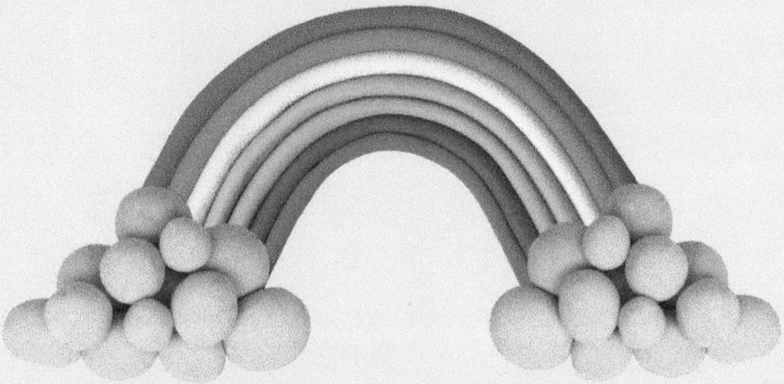

Rainbow

Rot

Red

Orange

Orange

Gelb

Yellow

Grün

Green

Blau

Blue

Indigo

Indigo

Violett

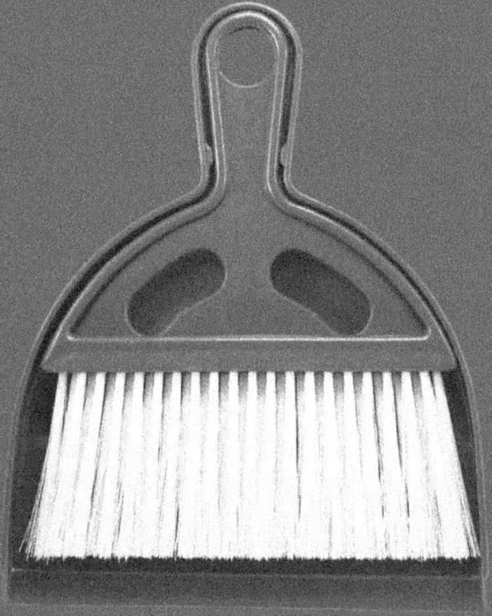

Violet

Oben

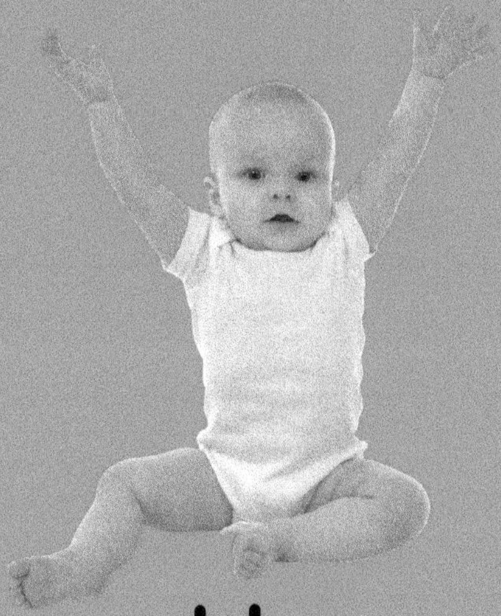

Up

Unten

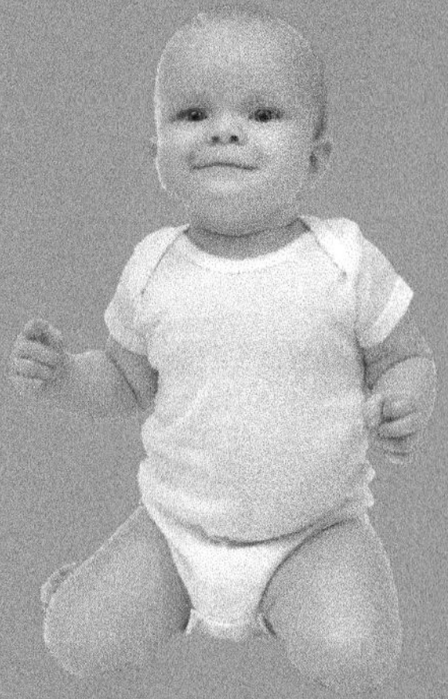

Down

Drinnen

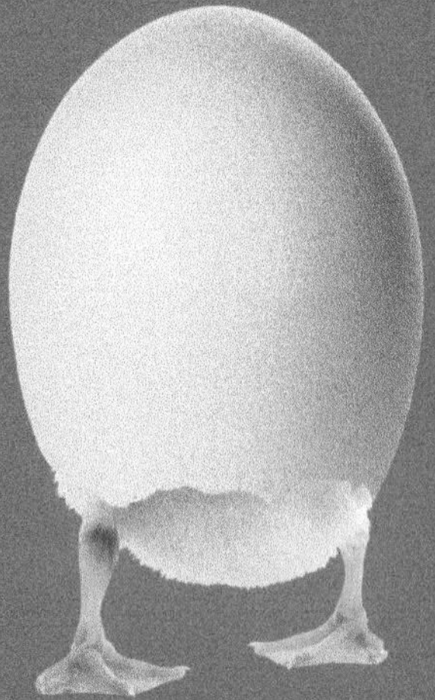

In

Draußen

Out

Heiß

Hot

Kalt

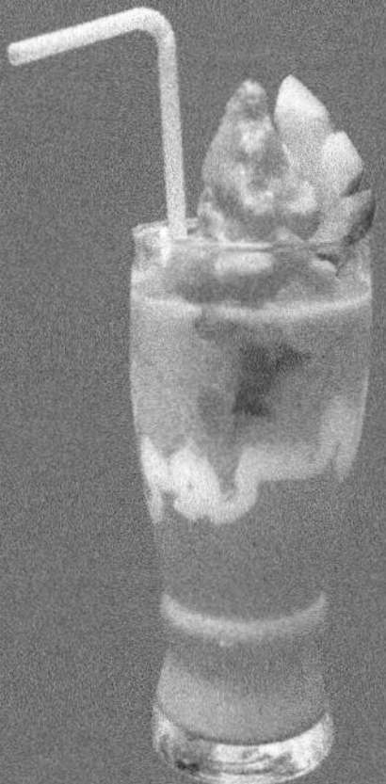

Cold

Nass

Wet

Trocken

Dry

Vorne

Front

Hinten

Back

An

On

Aus

Off

Offen

Open

Geschlossen

Closed

Leer

Empty

Voll

Full

Sicher

Safe

Gefährlich

Dangerous

Groß

Big

Klein

Small

Schlafend

Asleep

Wach

Awake

Lang

Long

Kurz

Short

der Kreis

Circle

das Quadrat

Square

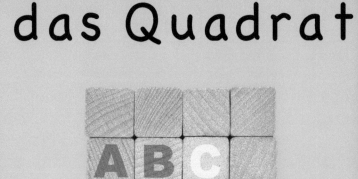

das Dreieck

Triangle

das Rechteck

Rectangle

das Karo

Diamond

der Stern

Star

das Oval

Oval

das Herz

Heart

Niesen

hatschi

Ah-choo

Sneeze

die Ente

Quak

Quack

Duck

die Kuh

Muh

Moo

Cow

das Telefon

Klingeling

Ring

Phone

der Affe

Ugh
ugh

Ooh-
ooh-
ahh-
ahh

Monkey

der Frosch

Quak

Ribbit

Frog

die Stille

Pst

Shh

Hush

der Hahn

Kikeriki

Cock-a-doodle-doo

Rooster

das Schlagzeug

Bumm

Boom

Drums

die Schlange

Zisch

Hiss

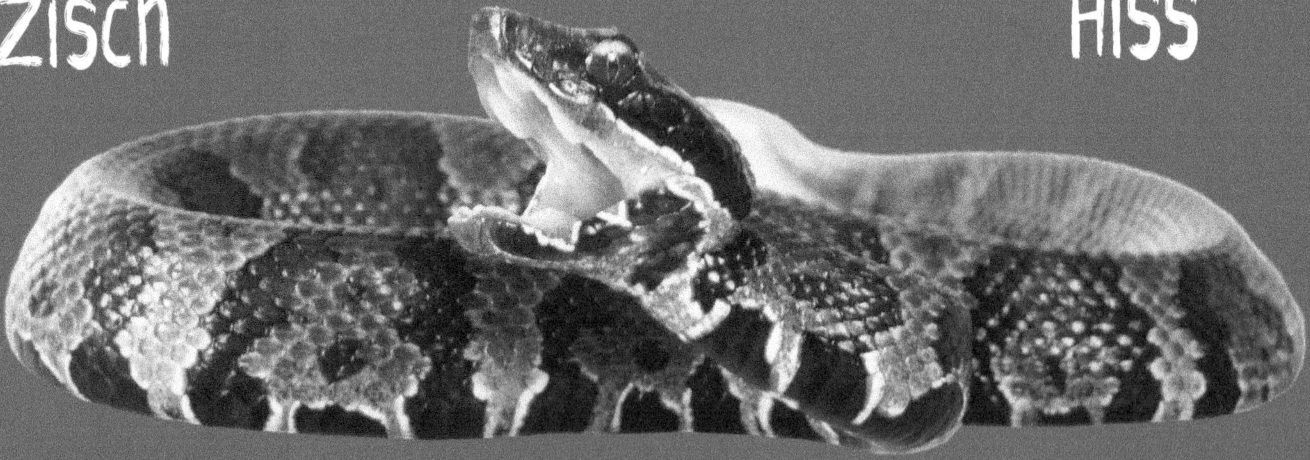

Snake

die Eule

Hu hu

Hoot

Owl

die Hummel

Summ

BUZZ

Bumblebee

die Hände

Klatsch

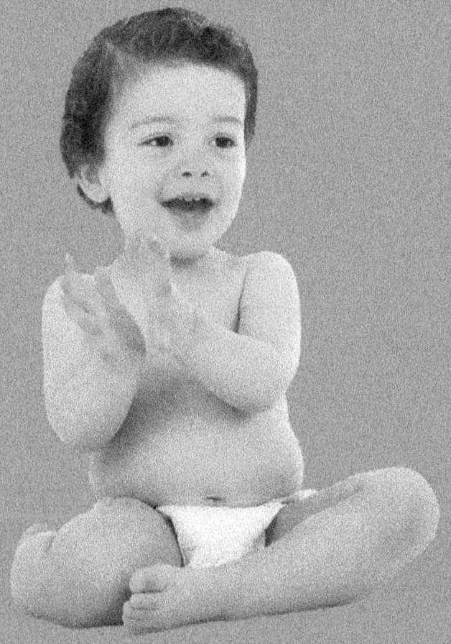

Clap

Hands

das Lamm

Mäh

Baa

Lamb

Kriechen

Crawl

Rollen

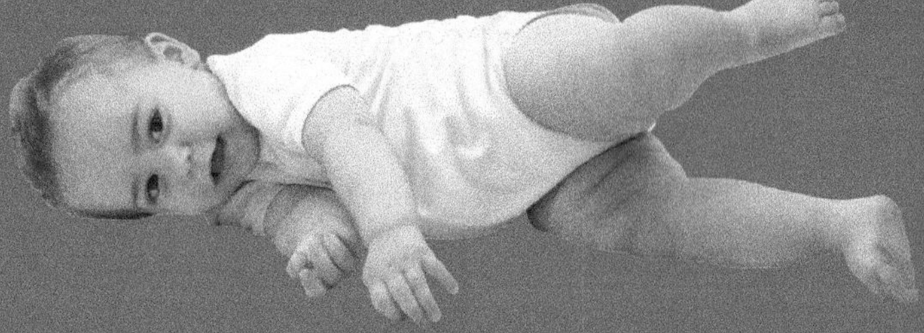

Roll

Gehen

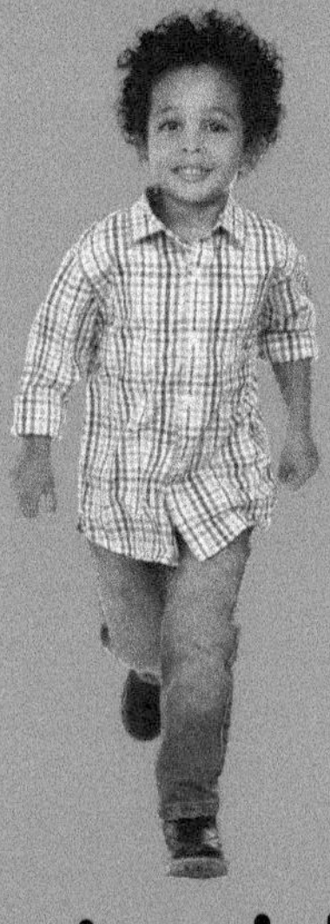

Walk

Rennen

Run

Hüpfen

Hop

Fahrrad fahren

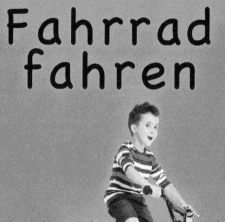

Ride

Küssen

Kiss

Springen

Jump

Fröhlich

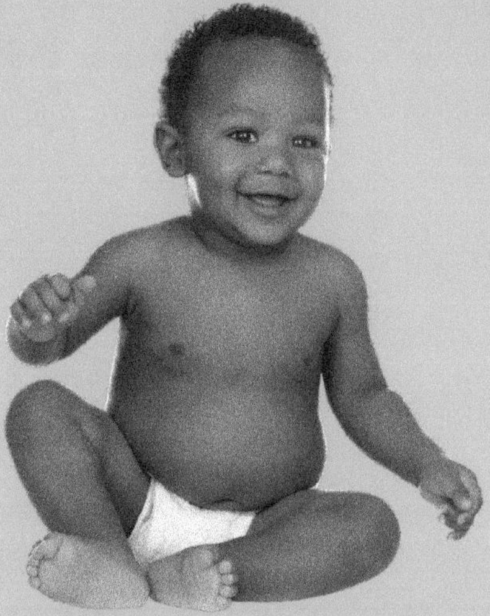

Happy

Traurig

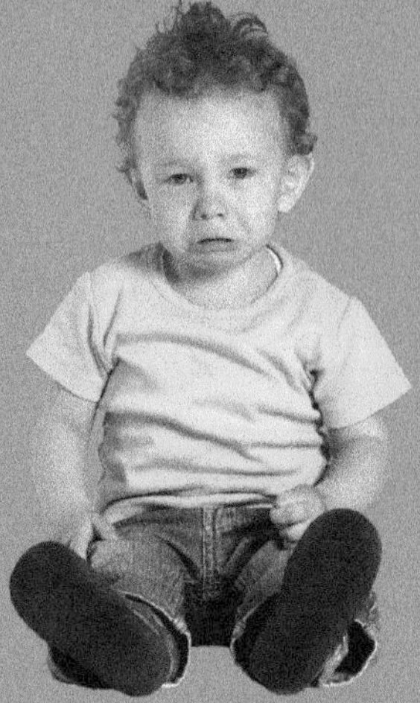

Sad

Ärgerlich

Angry

Ängstlich

Scared

Frustriert

Frustration

Überrascht

Surprise

Geschockt

Shock

Tapfer

Brave

Baseball

Baseball

Basketball

Basketball

Tennis

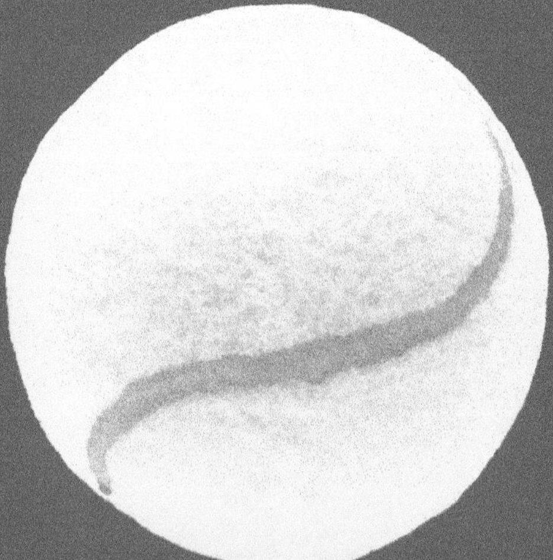

Tennis

Fußball

Soccer

Federball

Badminton

Football

Football

Volleyball

Volleyball

Golf

Golf

das Feuerwehrauto

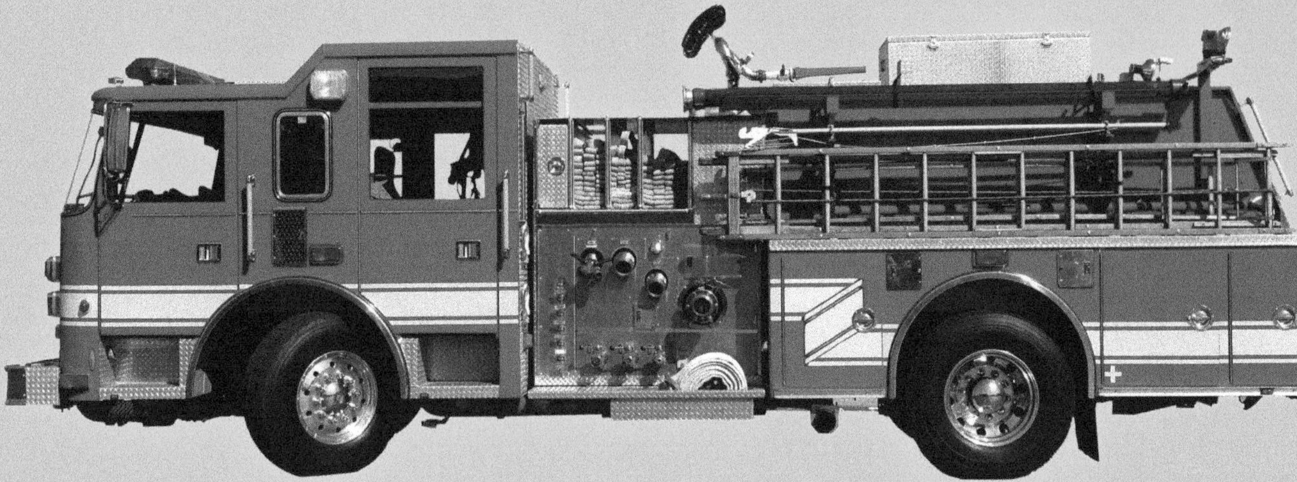

Fire truck

das Auto

Car

der Lastwagen

Truck

der Hubschrauber

Helicopter

das Flugzeug

Airplane

der Zug

Train

das Boot

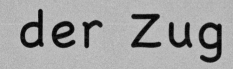

Boat

Klein Mittel Groß

Small Medium Large

Klein Mittel Groß

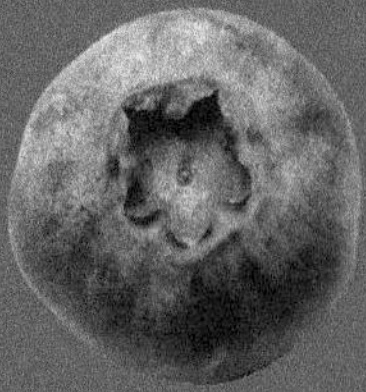
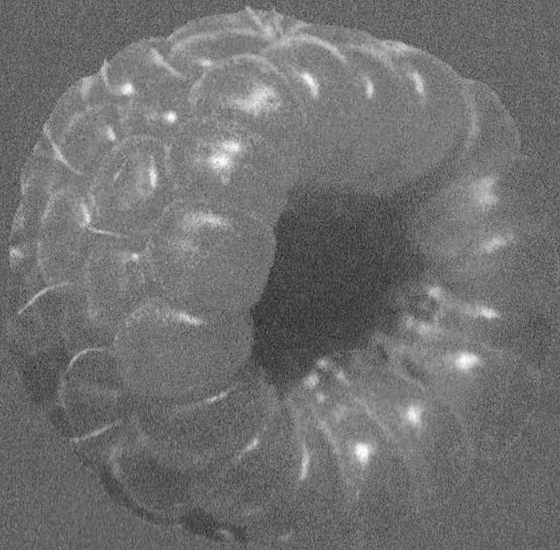

Small Medium Large

Groß Mittel Klein

Large Medium Small

Groß Mittel Klein

Large Medium Small

der Kopf

Head

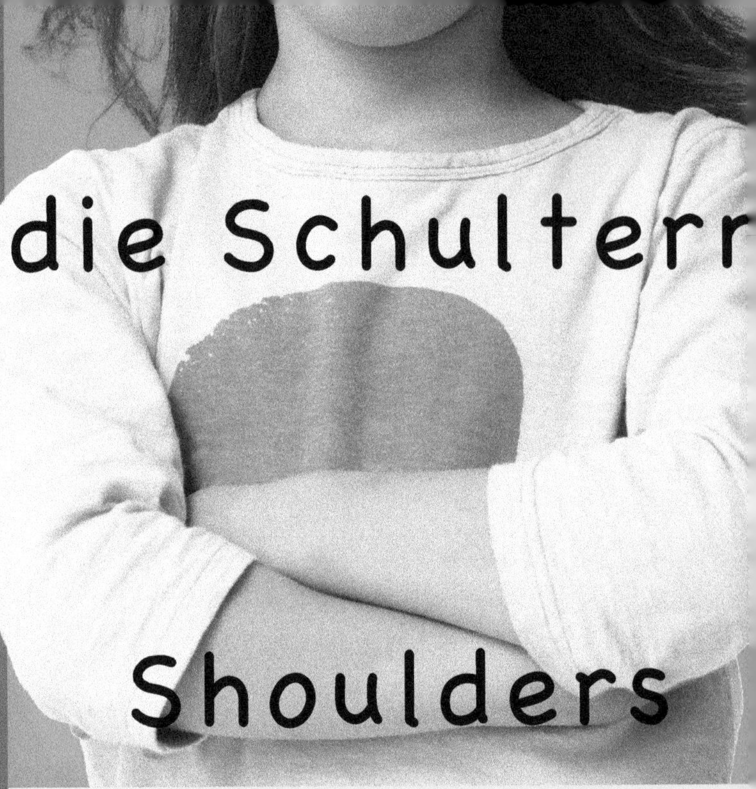

die Schulterr

Shoulders

die Knie

Knees

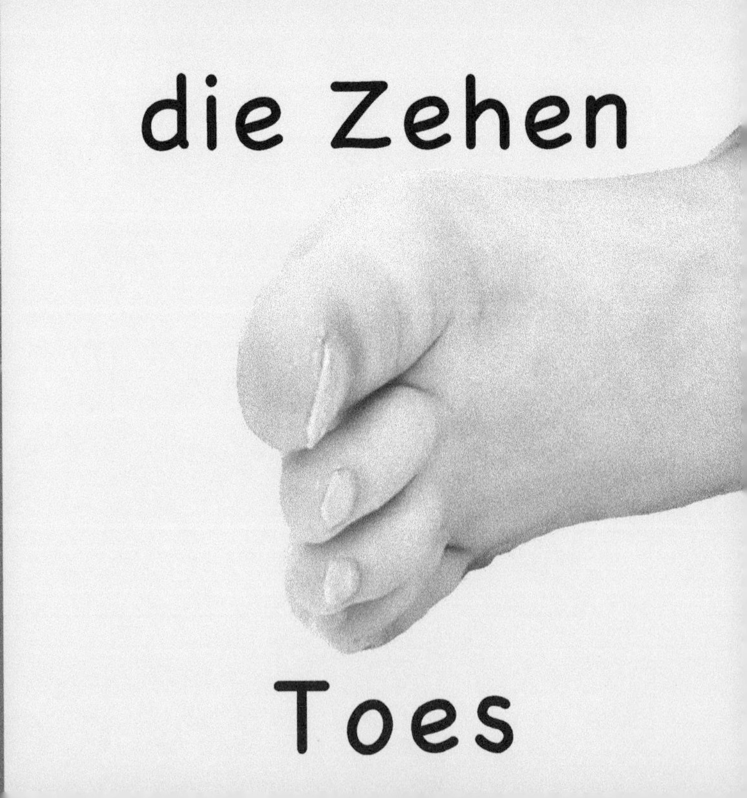

die Zehen

Toes

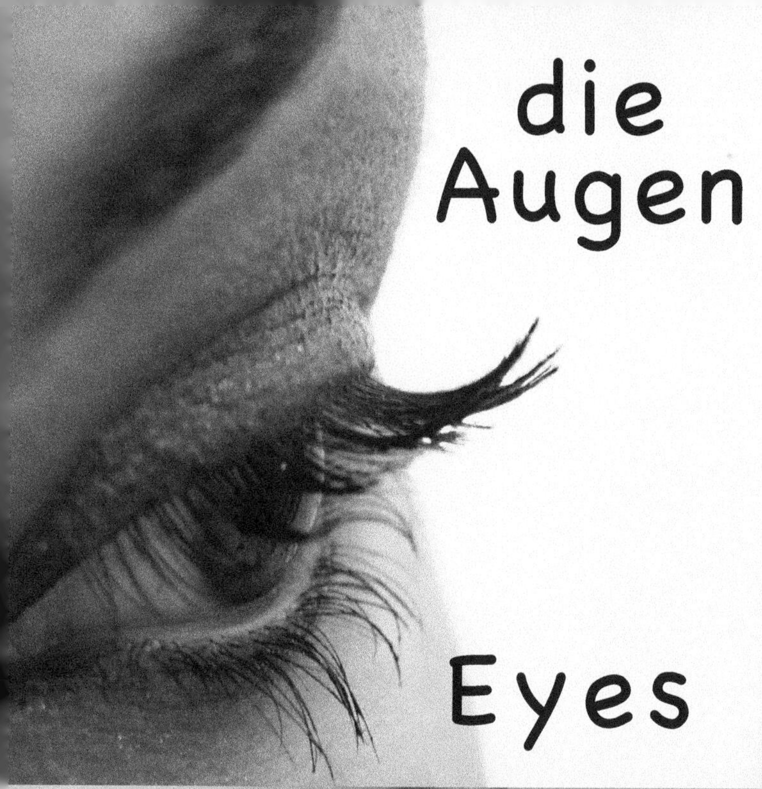
die
Augen
Eyes

die Ohren
Ears

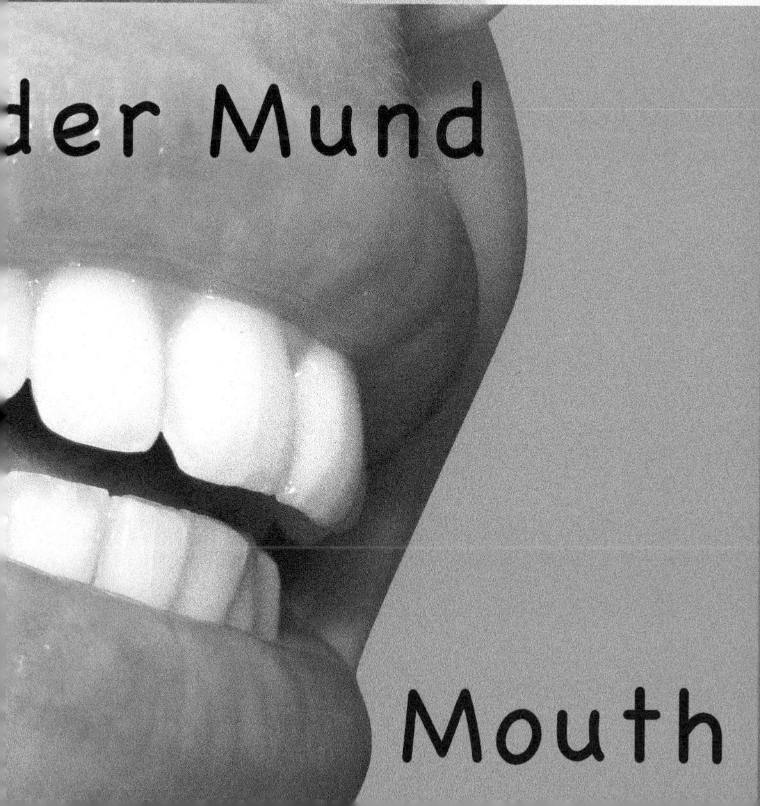
der Mund
Mouth

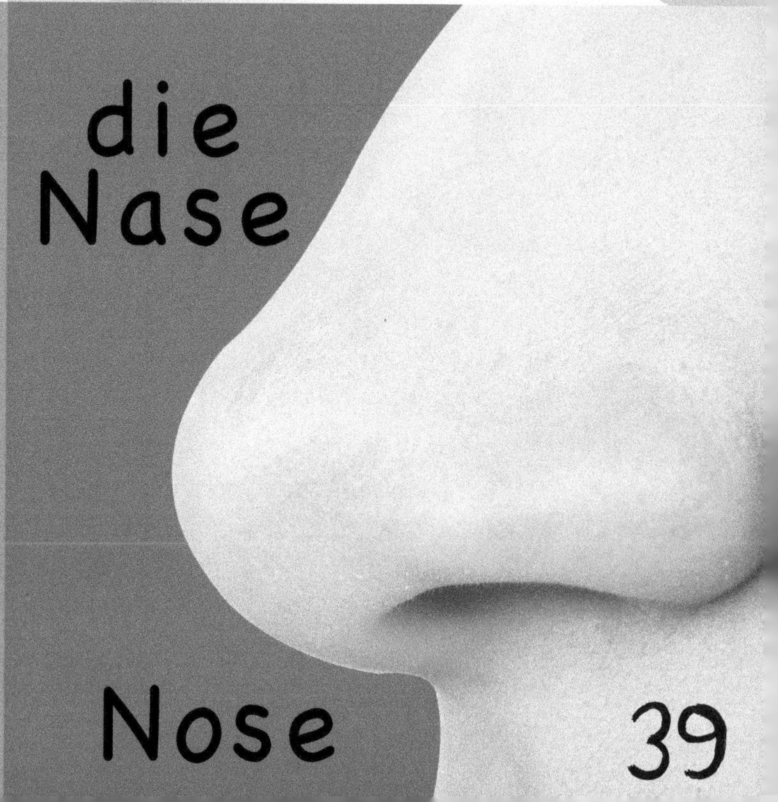
die
Nase
Nose

die Lerntasse

Sippy cup

die Schale

Bowl

der Topf

Pot

der Becher

Cup

der Teller

Plate

die Gabel

Fork

das Messer

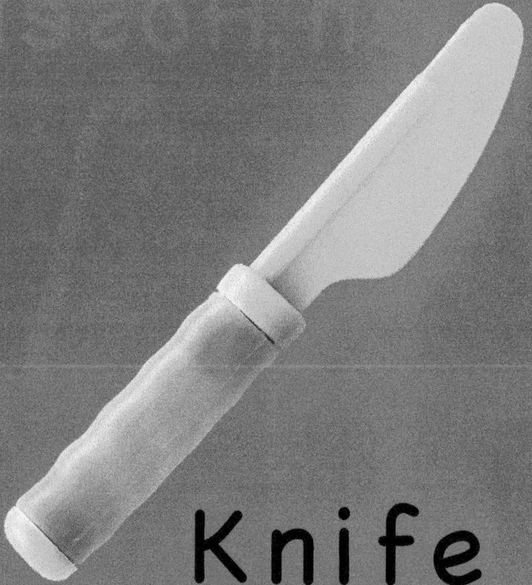

Knife

der Löffel

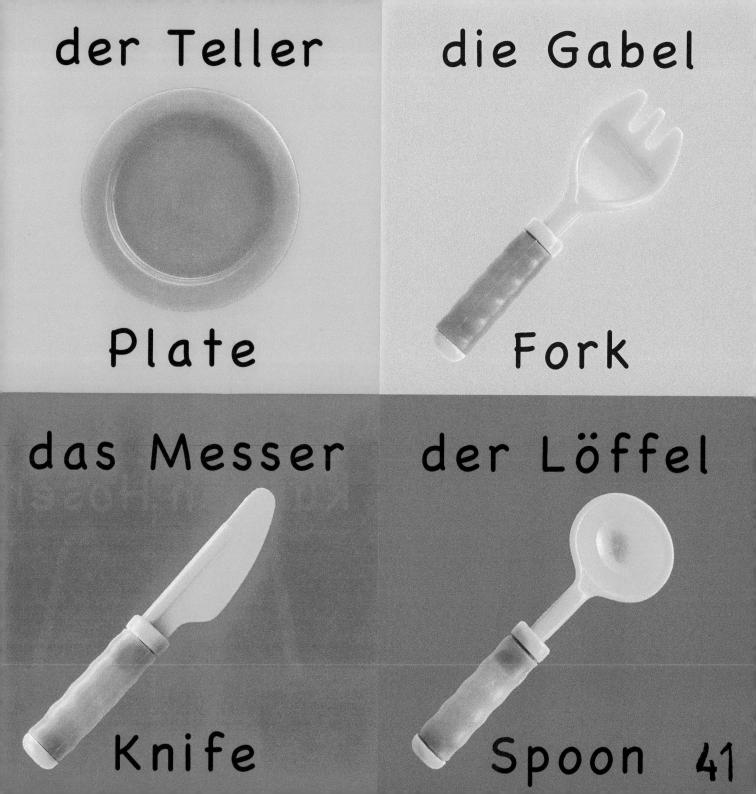

Spoon

der Hut

Hat

das Hemd

Shirt

die Hose

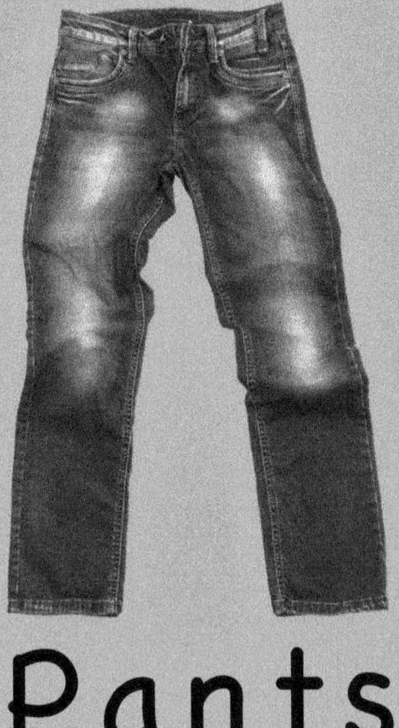

Pants

die kurzen Hosen

Shorts

die Handschuhe

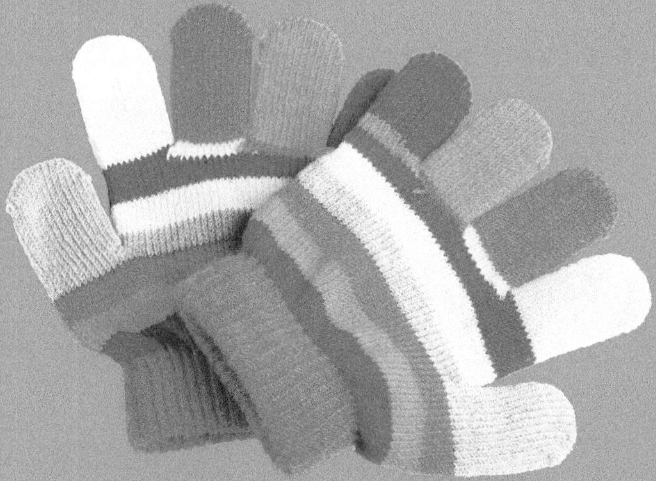

Gloves

die Sonnenbrille

Sunglasses

die Socken

Socks

die Schuhe

Shoes

die Badezeit
Bath time

die Badewanne

Bath

die Seife

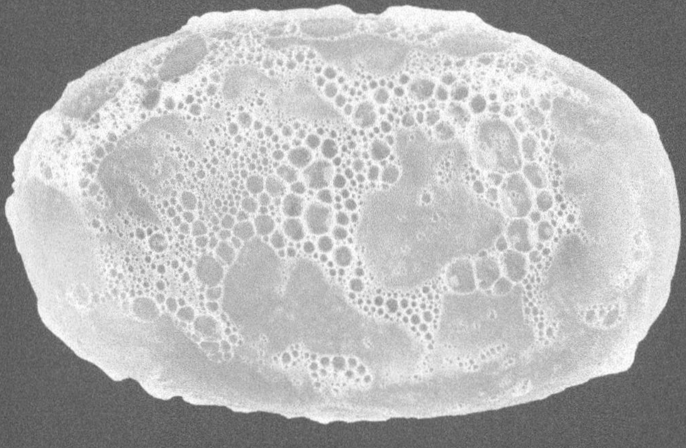

Soap

die Badeente

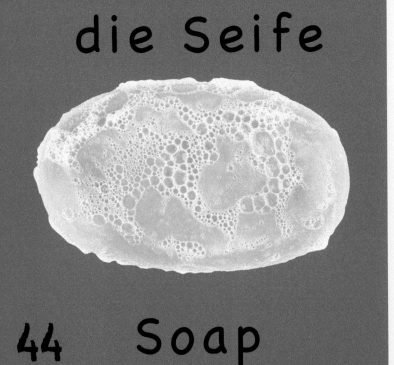

Rubber duck

Zähne putzen

Brush

die Schlafenszeit
Bed time

das Buch

Book

das Töpfchen

Potty

das Bett

Bed

THE TODDLER'S handbOOK

activity / Tätigkeit

Match the following to the pictures below. Can you find **7 pumpkins, a hooting owl, a rainbow, a baseball, a lion, a square, a sad boy, a helicopter, and shoes?**

Finde die passenden Bilder! Kannst du **7 Kürbisse, eine heulende Eule, einen Regenbogen, einen Baseball, einen Löwen, ein Quadrat, einen traurigen Jungen, einen Hubschrauber und ein Paar Schuhe** finden?

helicopter / der Hubschrauber

shoes / die Schuhe

hooting owl / die heulende Eule

baseball / der Baseball

7 pumpkins / 7 Kürbisse

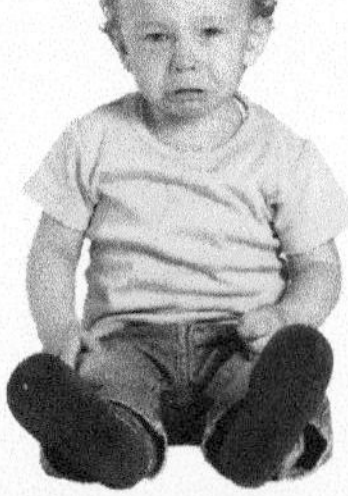

sad boy / der traurige Junge

lion / der Löwe

square blocks / ein Quadrat

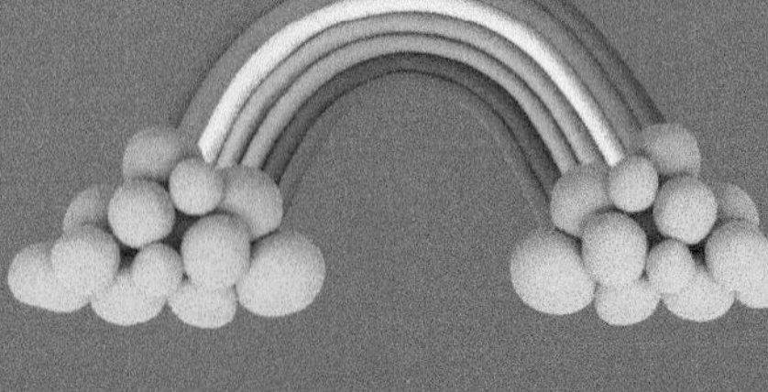

rainbow / der Regenbogen